House
World
Heaven

House
World
Heaven

Poems by

Edward A. Dougherty

© 2025 Edward A. Dougherty. All rights reserved.
This material may not be reproduced in any form, published,
reprinted, recorded, performed, broadcast,
rewritten, or redistributed without
the explicit permission of Edward A. Dougherty.
All such actions are strictly prohibited by law.

Cover design by Shay Culligan
Cover image by Richard Hendrick on Unsplash
Author photo by Beth Bentley

ISBN: 978-1-63980-968-4

Kelsay Books
502 South 1040 East, A-119
American Fork, Utah 84003
Kelsaybooks.com

Acknowledgments

I am deeply grateful to the editors of the following publications, where some of these poems first appeared, often in slightly revised form. These people frequently volunteer long hours on behalf of writers and readers.

Anterior Media: "Lost in the Garden," "The Heights of Ishizichi"
Brawl Lit: "Spruce Trees in the Rain"
Contemporary Haibun Online: "Matsuyama"
Friends Journal: "Setting Out"
Heliotrope: "Forsythia"
Kerf: "Mending the Earth," "Poem with No One in It," "How to Take It"
Manna: "A Room Full of Expectation"
Outside/In Literature and Travel Magazine: "When I Say 'Hiroshima'"
Parting Gifts: "Woodchip Path," "A Way Out," "Surrounding the Five Paragraph Essay"
Poets for a Livable Planet: "Strange Visitor"
Spire: "Real Spring"
Sunrise from Blue Thunder: "Yamadera"
Whetstone: "The Craft Studio"
The Whirlwind Review: "Kamakura"

"Fresh Brewed" and "After the State of the Union" first appeared in print on postcards created by Words on Wheels which delivered poetry to folks who were homebound in cooperation with Meals on Wheels. It turns out that the initiative launched in the spring of 2020, just as the COVID pandemic was shutting everything down, isolating us all. And yet, in the midst of that emergency, there was poetry, offering community.

C. J. Renz, O.P. gave *Small Galaxies* a careful, insightful reading, making superb suggestions, before publishing the chapbook in *Ruah*. The following poems appeared in that collection, which was granted the New Eden Chapbook Award: "Setting Out," "A Room Full of Expectation," "The Craft Studio," "Woodchip Path," "Bartimaeus," "Long Pilgrimage," "Saucer Magnolia," "Saint John," "Sequoia," "Taizé," "Eclipse," and "For Mtoto."

In addition to the larger literary community, honored in the many epigraphs and named in "Grace Street (II)," this poetic world could not have been built without the friendship of Steve Wilson, John Bradley, Scott Minar, and Ken Letko. Margaret Chula's detailed feedback enlivened the haibun in the Pilgrimage section, a gift for which I am grateful. This book may not be in the world had Margaret Reed not encouraged me to give it another chance, after I had put it aside; I am thankful for her faith in me, in these poems, and in her faith in the power of beauty to save us. I would not be the writer I am—the person I am—without Kate Dougherty's good influence, deep friendship, and spiritual companionship.

The same is true for Beth, whom I gratefully and happily share this luminous house with; she's been the love of my life from before we moved to Japan to this day when the poems about our return are published. This book is for her—they all are.

Contents

STORM WEATHER

Cold News	17
Morning, at the Table	19
At the Grocery	20
Fresh Brewed	22
The Routine	23
The Heart's Intentions	24
The Everyday Shames: Home Repairs	26
After the State of the Union	27
Storm Weather	28
How to Take It	30
Mortgage	31
Surrounding a 5-Paragraph Theme	33
The War at Home	34
A Way Out	35

RETREAT

Setting Out	39
Bartimaeus	40
A Room Full of Expectation	41
Long Pilgrimage	42
Saucer Magnolia	43
Sequoias	44
The Craft Studio	45
Taizé	46
Woodchip Path	47
Eclipse	48
For Mtoto	49

PILGRIMAGE

Arrivals and Departures	53
Yamadera	56
Kamakura	59
Lost in Gardens	65
Matsuyama	67
The Heights of Ishizuchi	71
When I Say 'Hiroshima'	73

REGROUNDING

Grace Street (II)	81

WIDE MIGRATIONS

False Spring	93
Forsythia	94
Strange Visitor	95
In the Desert	96
Mending the Earth	99
A Poem With No One in It	100
The Search for Avalon	101
Real Spring	102
The Circuit	103
For the Autumn Equinox	105
Spruce Trees in Rain	108
Autumn Songs	109
Listening to Snow	110
Snowfields	113
For the Winter Solstice	115

STORM WEATHER

sometimes he starts in his slumber
and wonders at himself and his house

and muses strangely
　　　at the resemblance
　　　　　betwixt him and it

—Ralph Waldo Emerson

Cold News

—i—

With frost crackling
like radio waves, the paperboy
trudges through icy dawn.
A truck in low gear, morning
groans, straining against the dark.

—ii—

No malice. An accident:
another hunter sensed motion
and sprayed the far woods.
At the hospital, the wounded man
hallucinates:
          In dazzling white,
his daughter floats up the aisle
to his best friend,
the one who shot him. He dreams
the sanctuary flickers with wings.

—iii—

Where is the place for the balloon-faced man
who weaves his bike through downtown
in short sleeves? Once the library opens,
it can be his home against the elements,
but for these blue hours, he rides. Brown snowpiles
shimmy his wheels. He nearly wipes out
waving to the bookstore owner
who in her still-dark shop
pours the first pitcher of water into the coffee maker.

—iv—

The paperboy snaps open
the outer door, drops on the porch
the day's hard news,
moves on down the block
stomping across the year.

Morning, at the Table

We begin where we are: at Beth's thrift shop table
which I love, surrounded by books, a bottle of ink,
small paintings I made and do not understand.

While I sip coffee, a woman in Guatemala
cannot sleep from the aching song her bones
and muscles and skin have started to hum

having picked bean by bean the coffee I drink,
having roused her girl from hammock-shaped earth
between rows, having carried her home,

eaten, laid her down again, stretched herself out,
and now as the sun rises once more
faces her work in the fields again.

In my dream, I shuffle through carpeted,
cubicled hallways. Each handshake
a smiling betrayal, eye confronting eye,

when identity peels away like calendar pages
flip, flip, flip and we age into another version
leaving something behind, something forever gone,

we also gather up what cannot be lost.
My cup is empty. The house here is quiet.
The day soars out like a hillside

blushing with ripe beans, and as it does
part of the world slips into darkness, toward a time
to sink into the power and the life,
into that which endures.

At the Grocery

In the airy, bright supermarket café,
I sit, my coffee's too-strong bitterness
telling me about the hole it's got to be

burning through my stomach. For a long time,
I take a cup, as I do every day,
and for a long time, I sit in my coat,

just sit, coffee cooling as I recall
the worn plank floor of the grocery store
in a town so different now that I'm sure

I wouldn't even know it, probably
wouldn't like it. Over the door, a hooked bell
rang sweet and long when people entered.

The cool was not conditioned air, but shade,
and it took eyes a while to get used to.
The old woman in a white apron would turn

finally from the musical, mechanical
cash register and greet you. Her face was pinched,
and whiskers grew on her chin and lip,

some sprouting from a mole along her nose.
I'm older now than she was then, and I know now
that work—repetitive, heavy labor—

will do that to you: leave you lingering
over a strong but remote memory
and a cardboard cup of specialty coffee

for no reason. I know now that time too
can be made bitter, so strong it eats holes
in anything that tries to hold it.

Fresh Brewed

Cup of decaf, a plate of eggs.
A couple of counter-stool pundits
expound on what makes this country great
while Faye races to get more rye
toasted. *Is it dry, Mike?*
It's got to be dry.

At a booth, grandparents teach
manners: *what do you say?*
when Faye brings the little girl
her glass of juice, then
when the meal comes, *now,*
they prompt her, *put the game away.*

It's time to eat. It's the work
of being human, community labor
that builds something durable,
a structure larger and sturdier
than the self. My cup's full again,
steaming, without my even asking.

Of course, that part may be commerce,
paid work, service and goods
exchanged for currency, but Faye smiles
and jokes that the pot's fresh-
squeezed and the counter-men
stop discussing the hunting season
to laugh and ask if the OJ
was brewed just that morning.

The Routine

From the west
              the wind blurs
reddening my eyes. A blue jay

commands
              a wire-full of doves
to move on, and I—
              a grey smudge
walking of a morning—remain

to witness the man
              pound the door
at the housing project—five a.m.—and announce

the routine:
              it's fumigation day.
She must gather up
              the kids,
any perishables,
              and get out. Stay away
at least until dinnertime.

Today, the sky
              cannot hold
all of its blue, and the buses,

all the buses are running late.

The Heart's Intentions

—i—Simone

*When I met her
in a drug rehabilitation center
she was trying to become
drug free so she could*

*join the Job Corps,
finish high school, and obtain
some vocational training.*

'I want to be a model.
I want to have a Jacuzzi.
I want to have a big
BIG house and a BIG family—
three girls and two boys.'

'And what about the man?'

'He'll be a lawyer. He'll be
responsible, hard-working,
and sensitive to my feelings.
Everything will be fifty-fifty.
And he'll take the boys out
to play football. I'll have the girls
inside cooking. That would be
a dream come true!'

—ii—Jacqueline

Nineteen, pregnant
with her fourth.
                Afraid

of losing her partner,
of ending up
alone.

      When he gets
drinking again
or shooting up

she's wise enough
to the heart's
                good intentions

to know a solution.
However temporary.
He'll stay
       for the baby.

She wants a job
               —a good one.
Who can blame her? She wants
to be able to read the paper.

Part one is a found poem from Ruth Sidel's On Her Own: Growing Up in the Shadow of the American Dream

The Everyday Shames: Home Repairs

I brood on the uselessness of letters.
—Tu Fu

Talking to men like Henry
whose muscles outline his thin frame
more than the years, none
of the little machines I've constructed

seem to matter. He worked
over at the concrete factory
until a bigger outfit bought it out
and had no more use

for him. Now he fixes mowers
and sells them from his garage.
It's clear he's been listening to engines
all his life, can tell *the seal's broke*

from the sound of it. In the darkness
long before the rest of us are up,
he hauls stacks of papers in his van
to deliver them on the porch
of this disinterested literacy.

After the State of the Union

Some days you need to order
breakfast where a perfect stranger
calls you "Hon," where regulars
take their mugs outside
to stand around the newspaper machine,
smoking, where you pour sugar
from pillar canisters and yank
your own napkins from dispensers
right on the table. Slowly, snow hardens
under the weight of the cold.
The sky's the color of the smokers' breath.
The eggs come dry, the homefries salty.
Wheat toast, in four triangles,
comes piled point to point.
When the guy at the end of the counter
calls out, "You've got friends in low places,"
you almost get up to take the stool beside him.
The regulars will tell you everything
you already know about the government
but say it anyway. You can count on it.
A bottomless cup of coffee for a buck
is sometimes all it takes to stay sane.

Storm Weather

—i—

Ruthless and vain,
the rain stops
at nothing. It rests
then returns.
In its slanting spirals
is piano music—

but a roof-joint
could crash
and crush everything
you've stored in the rooms
of your sympathy.

No more to say
of this weather's
potential for sorrow
except:

the motion's lovely
slashing
across the linden tree.

—ii—

There's more to this story, I'm sure of it,
something about her boyfriend's forecast,
which includes threats of violence.

I'm real sorry, she said, *but I gotta drop out.
I can't come to school anymore.*
Then she headed out—

no raincoat, no umbrella,
only her fine, taut voice.

How to Take It

You are deciding how much you can take,
whether he is sorry enough this time, and he is
as he always is and as you always grant him
because you know what you seem to lose.
You know things could get worse, and not only the car.

I'm not telling you anything you don't already carry with you
past that cemetery every day, its stones like teeth,
some crooked, some preserved, some knocked down.
You feel sorry for them
because you know how to take it.

You've stopped thinking about them as signs
with people's names gouged right out of the stone.
Markers tell the bare facts of a life like a landlord
who says *Yeah, they used to live here . . .*
but nothing more, not *The little one,*
she had asthma and a wonderful giggle.

Something's been carved out of you these last years
—all that pounding—
but what's the message you send?

It's a question you ask, touching up your makeup,
a question you don't answer
because you're going to be late for work
and the kids aren't yet at daycare
and the day slips away which makes him mad.
It's a question you don't want to answer
because you can
and because that old cemetery is already full.

Mortgage

—i—Inspection

He points to the main service
and I picture the water,
white with force, turning
the great turbine,
says *This isn't good,*
see this one's
triple tapped
            and a mountain
in southeast Kentucky shudders
and here's no ground wire,
none at all
           all day
the fire burns and it burns
all through the night
but you should be alright
with 60 amps
           and the rods
of nearly pure uranium
descend into their slots,
the meter tipping.

—ii—Interest

Once you divvy up
all that money over all those years
and to all the people involved
what's $192,000

                As if things weren't connected
like the clouds over New Mexico
and the great hope of the people under them
as the rain continues not to fall
and the winds continue to rage
and the wildfires go on burning
                                    unless you can't
fill a prescription for an always-redfaced
daughter   crying now for two days
she says *you can't go to no drugstore*
with no money

Surrounding a 5-Paragraph Theme

A soldier can make her family proud
by getting out of a rotting town, a set of fields
that might make a life
but not a living; she can learn

a skill, earn respect, travel
to countries ruled by bowls of rice
or prayer five times a day, places where
for the cost of a used car,

everything's available on the free market:
anthrax in a sealed envelope, a thimbleful
of sarin. When our soldier comes down
with unexplained cancer, she no longer knows

who the enemy is. Our soldier travels home,
having been discharged (honorably),
and enrolls at the community college
where she writes an essay.

The War at Home

Her feet ache as she opens the door to her small house, the now alone house full of tiny glass animals, stuffed angels with blue wings, and dresser-top gnomes with little laughing faces. She sighs and wants another life, not hers, not the humiliation of a co-worker who says, "Oh, I *guess* you could use *that* form," not the degrading indirection. She walks through the living room, late spring sun coating the recliner and sofa with amber. She tosses her keys in a bowl on the kitchen table, sits down and begins sheafing her mail. Last night,

dreaming, she drove to the grocery store, rehearsing her list—*mayonnaise, ten-penny nails, shoelaces (not the waxed kind), and a sixpack of beer* (as she drove, she felt the relief of being able to have a few bottles safely in the house again)—the sound of thunder all around her. In the wheel, a shaking like an earthquake (even dreaming she noted the lack of logic: *how's she know what an earthquake feels like?*). Was a tractor trailer about to crest the hill behind her (*on this prairie highway?*)? Would it crush her little car before the driver even knows she's there? *What makes such a sound?* She scans what sky she can see up through the top of the windshield,

out through the driver's window for the warplane the newscaster called a Warthog. The roaring, rumbling, aching now in her arms and belly, shoulders and chest the sound was only getting closer, closer, approaching her, targeting her in that tiny blue car as she raced to reach the border, if only she could cross in time . . .

A Way Out

—i—

Take Fifth Street
past the crumbling drug house
to the train tracks
Follow them   They're hardly used
When you get to the river
now you've got to choose

—ii—

Fumigating
at the Section 8 housing
begins at 5 a.m. In the paper,
dollar-and-no-
nonsense logic.

—iii—

A burning house. Photos
of the amusement park,
long closed, become
grey ash. This place

is a shipwreck, everybody
for themselves. Head off
by yourself—if you get close enough
they'll pull you under.

—iv—

The highway's
a vein of fire

Take it   Drive
almost to the cliff-face

—that earthen cooler
where once a brewery
stored its kegs—

The cloverleaf
will direct you

What you need's
on the wind

Time to learn
to move with it

RETREAT

Prayer is the mortar that holds our house together.
—Teresa of Avila

The ground of the soul is dark.
—Meister Eckhart

One should identify oneself with the universe itself.
—Simone Weil

Setting Out

Beginnings have their own success

like snowfall: the clarity that something
is finally moving. This time

it's you. Are you drawn
by a more promising field, or squeezed
until leaving's the only way
to stay whole? Maybe

you've cracked open,
growing too large for old forms,
growing even now
in the white heart of winter.

In any case, you stand shaking
in the momentous world.

A black-capped chickadee
navigates the crab-apples' tangle
to land and feed:

do you believe in birds only
when they are visible?

The whiteness of snow
is a kind of emptiness

you fully understand.

Bartimaeus

Mark 10:46–52

Stone chips and pebbles
speckle the low mud wall.

Only a few hours of shade
before the summer sun
brazes his skin to blisters.

Sound of the crowd reaches him
long before any dust
or condemnation.

He could see once,
hold a job, have a place
in the circles
of economy and community.

Why cry out first
for pity? Attention?
Being recognized
as a human being?

There's no suspense here:
Jesus restores his sight.
But before that,

in the haze of dust, the stink
of hot bodies
stalled beside an earthen wall,

there is this stark moment—

*What do you want me
to do for you?*

A Room Full of Expectation

In the winter, when snow fell by the foot, there was dancing in this room. Laughing circles. Legs and arms, music and languages from many countries all turning around and around while the world outside managed itself as it always does. This is a roomful of breathing. A cargo of expectation. It would be easy to say, "Half is lit, but the whole is in the Light," but darkness, like these whitewashed bricks, surrounds us. We were asked to recall exemplars, and stories swelled the room with all the invisible ones who urged us on to this moment. The father in the front of the boat, holding steady. An old woman who went out to share in the gathering so she wouldn't die in her hogan, saving the family the burden of burning it to the ground. A writer working in fits and starts between child tending and dozing off in the vast, silent sanctuaries after midnight, and her book contains a truth that now lives in one of us years later. The mentor whose very life was a comfort, even when he himself didn't know it. These spirits gathered in this bare room as they always do; not speaking is one part of our response. In candlelight, the walls seem softer, more like a body than a building, and that night of dancing we were living inside it. Sitting and breathing together becomes part of that larger life. This is always true, of course, but that night, another part of us woke up to it. A space opened in us, as wisdom does. We were living in our larger self, and a small white room was breathing inside us.

Long Pilgrimage

Like any other dining hall, the usual rectangular tables surrounded by wooden chairs are the setting for familiar customs of sharing food. Between meals, though, the room holds a strange repose, a quiet like my schooldays' kitchen after the dishwasher finished churning. I'd spread my textbooks across the table to do my homework while another part of me stared from the night-blank windows. Those were the days I learned that *the longest journey is the journey inwards.* I think of the prophet Elijah running off to Mount Sinai when the king wanted to kill him. On foot, he traveled days through the wilderness to finally fling himself, exhausted, on the hard ground. There he slept. An angel woke him, and by his head Elijah found bread and a jar of water. "It will be a long journey," the angel told him. He ate then dozed again. A second time, the angel woke him up with the same message, the same gifts. Because his life's at stake, he did as he's told. Elijah was renewed enough to climb the sacred mountain and face the God of the Universe, who sweeps by in the small whispering sound. The dining room is a shrine dedicated to such long pilgrimages, such transformations. How leaves of spinach or lettuce grow eyes in us. Olives, crushed to oil and sent across oceans, gain legs and, in us, walk the earth. At mealtimes, the dining space fills with motion and randomness. Bearing their trays before them, diners head for the side table for drinks or scan faces for that sign of hospitality. Glad to be useful, plates and glasses and silver are unafraid to make sound. Each table becomes a small galaxy. Each of us is created from material issued from stars that collapsed so intensely the fundamental nature of those elements changed.

Saucer Magnolia

Pink was never a soft, girlie-girlie color to these trees, but life-and-death. Beauty's a matter of survival. Someone said we take all the wrong things seriously, and this is one of them. I want to say something so we won't deny or forget such power even though most words blow away soon after falling to the ground. I am dying a little with every blossom. A group of us stretched out on the grass before the thick petals began raining down and read Mark's Gospel aloud, hearing in human voices our own harshness, stupidity, and possibility. The sky's always been this blue. Daffodils, tulips, cherry trees always break into beauty after winter. I am becoming something, but I can't know what yet.

Sequoias

Like sisters who gather over coffee because one of them has found a lump in her breast, these three redwoods are straggled and lovely. A lost species growing right here in suburbia. Sometimes you have to go all the way to China—which they did to "discover" these trees—to find that rough elegance within you the whole time. All winter, hanging in their high branches, tangled in their hair: Venus, that evening star which is not a star but a planet whose features are all named for women. It has something to do with endurance, which for most of us would be enough. There's a certain grace in naming things appropriately: redwood/redbud, tree/tumor, malignant/benign. Where branches push out of the trunk, a kind of teardrop crevice forms, as if growing in one place takes something from somewhere else. That's why standing together makes all the difference. Over the years, the moon whitewashes everything with romance, but the sisters endure. April comes again and the redwoods put out tiny, soft needles like green fans.

The Craft Studio

The wheels spin like my mind in silence. Paper remembers the flow of sap, exchange of sunlight into sugar. The tables are high, closer to the heart. Another room dedicated to transformation. Clay becomes plates and bowls and shapes it takes two hands to discover. Once I lost myself in mixing colors, slipping into each other, becoming new shades. Watercolors are like tears in a still puddle, like sunrise, like the secret gestures of incense. Paint floated and mixed as if it forgot who it was and only when the soggy card stock dried did the pigment come to its senses. Isn't this what we do when we fall in love? When we learn in our age about a Texas town where a black man is dragged behind a pickup truck to his death? This is the necessity of the Craft Studio. Vivaldi or Albinoni giving rhythm to the whole room, the large windows, the looms idly dreaming of streams of wool, the shelves protecting their unfinished projects. What happens when a person gets lost in the shaping of material? All I know is there is an emptying that comes with creation, a forgetting that must be acted out, a magnetic reorientation that spins you in the right direction.

Taizé

Taizé is a river valley breaking into all the shades of green to bear witness to the power of greening. Taizé is a gathering of people, an abbey, a movement. A way of prayer. A flock of birds moving as one, all heading to a place they know by feel. Each voice begins by gathering air, soul, soil. In this drawing in, there is France and England, the States and Germany, Argentina and Laos. There is a steppe with sweetgrass growing waist high, smelling like rain. There is a mountain slope so steep and cragged that it is no longer beautiful but it is beautiful. Taizé is a line of poplars, unmoving and swaying, so green they are black from a distance. And Taizé is the first solo voice lifting out from the trees and the rest of the flock, rising to fly through the radiant, green valley.

Woodchip Path

Sometimes when walking the path along the southeast, you can't tell what's traffic and what's wind in the needles. Mostly it's the highway, newly laid down but laid out in minds and meetings for decades. In the time between decision and dynamite, green spaces throughout the area slipped away, and are now like the faces of the dead which are so familiar and so lost. There are times when tears come burning: the mind suddenly grasps how far away these lovers have moved. The heart has always understood this distance. Mostly, though, it's a sound like the surf, a sighing in the spruce trees, a moan in the pines. One day a woodchuck lumbering across, all fur and wobble. A few days before, rain pounded down, briefly and completely. The water carved a rivulet in the path as it pushed the chips aside or carried them down the hill, where the woodchuck headed. At night, when leaving the open Firbank Field and entering the embrace of trees planted by men who refused to go to war, the sky collapses under the canopy of branches and is as far away as surf pounding the shore. Woodchips piled by the cartload cannot cover up the beating pulse of the earth under our feet. The chips themselves contain a spark of the trees which once knew the vitality of soil. The heart understands this; that's why the path takes such care and so much work. Each step is a memorial to what is passing, to what is past, to what is possible, and to what is emerging. Each step is a leaving behind and an arrival.

Eclipse

What is this we call sin? Is it like Bindweed vining through the garden, the plant you spend hours ripping out but still is all you see, tangling and undesirable? The eclipsed moon rose over the line of pines, over the garden and Firbank Field. We huddled together pointing out the Dog Star, took the Pleiades eye-test, and watched as the moon changed from a rose in the black sky back to its familiar face. The night was soft around us as March blew through into April. And belief? Is faith drawing connections in the scattered and distant stars whose light comes to us only later? Now a bear, now a mother and child. Is it a map we hold to the night sky to seek the shapes that are out there whether we recognize them yet or not? We sang all the moon-songs we could remember, raising our voices with all the romantics who've gone before: heads tipped back to that white disk floating in the world beyond, the world above, the world all around us. And I, too, return again and again to it, finding it in the square of window facing east. And I keep coming back, circling, revisiting the face of the mind that rounds and wanes like the moon which rose red and filled like a bowl with milk. *God is a mother,* someone once said, *who gives us the universe to suckle.*

For Mtoto

Your eyes, Child, are dark waters, still and deep. They receive the sky as it collapses into us, receive the green trees as they leaf out into towering beings guarding us all. Your eyes take us in. For a year now you've shifted from hip to hip, from one stranger to another, but you will not remember us. We've passed through you like a fragrance. But you, Child, you who watched us, who drew from us our desire to delight, you have become something sure and firm in us. You have been carried off to New Zealand where the sea whispers a lullaby all day and long into the night. Child, you have been cherished away to Europe where there are castles and cities like every other city, but you, alert and watchful, have been slipped into a small country of silence. You've been cradled into the mountains of South America where the air becomes so thin people gasp for it like love, where the soil slips to the sea and you, Child, will watch this migration. Can I say you are the body of Christ taken whole and understood only in part, understood in as many ways as you are taken. In us you are always young, Child. But in you, we have passed through like rain, and anything you remember will have to be given to you again by someone else. We who pass like shadows on the wall remember you as you grow up in a place we cannot imagine. But we imagine you there.

PILGRIMAGE

Out in the field, a horse, and nearby a man cutting grass. I stopped to ask directions. Courteous, he thought awhile then said, "Too many intersecting roads. It's easy to get lost. Best to take that old horse as far as he'll go. He knows the road. When he stops, get off, and he'll come back alone."

—Matsuo Basho in *Oku no Hosomichi*

Travel is a meditation because we must constantly inquire: Where am I? What is this? And this? *The jolt of foreignness can spur awakening—flooding us with change, that mark of existence we often don't notice in our daily lives. The truth is, we're always traveling, always in flux.*

—Anita N. Feng

Arrivals and Departures

In moving through new landscapes, we travel through ourselves as well. No matter if it's mountains wreathed in the mists of mystery or lonely bus stops or ultra-modern train stations, foreign landscapes invite us to face our response to the world. In this way, travel is like poetry.

One summer, I returned to Japan after a decade away. My spouse and I had been volunteers at a Hiroshima peace center, where we lived and worked for two and a half years. Making no regular income allowed little time for sightseeing. Therefore, this return journey would mix tourism with pilgrimage and reunion. It all began with a dislocating mix of bad movies and bland food on a 13-hour flight.

> patient, the little girl
> licks and licks the cream center
> of her Oreo

✧

> straddling the seats' gap
> I view the mountains below
> —your body is warm

✧

> descending through clouds
> the huge engine disappears—
> when will we see land

Returning to Japan allowed us to visit places in the north, famous temples and gardens, and even hike the highest mountain on the island of Shikoku. Every place we encounter—from our kitchen to a world-famous statue—layers itself within us with impressions, hearsay, and memory, so it takes special effort to free ourselves and encounter the place itself and not our idea of it. Such immediacy requires inner availability and spaciousness. Because I've traveled to many of these sites before in books, such openness was often elusive for me.

> walking with giants
> Basho, Saigyo, and Shiki—
> lands printed with poems

૪

Our plane circled Narita for over an hour before we filed through immigration, baggage claim, and customs. By the time we got to the *midori-no-madoguchi,* the Green Window, it was about to close and flooded with customers. We didn't know about the typhoon that stranded all of these travelers.

We had been fed breakfast in the air—awful eggs and watery coffee—but we were hungry anyway. The body understands time in its own way. At a stand in the terminal, we bought a couple of *onigiri.* I thought again how these triangles of rice are like sandwiches, only the lunch meat could be fish or vegetables, the bread's rice, and lettuce seaweed. "Like," only in concept. Then we lugged our baggage outside the airport to catch the hotel's shuttle bus.

asleep on our feet
we munch our *onigiri*
and watch the rain fall

Yamadera

Our first stop was Yamagata, a city well north of Tokyo . . .

I don't want to tick off activities, an agenda to get through. What I did or saw. In life as in poetry, we want mood and nuance. We want a moment to enlarge with implication so it can include the past and suggest the future. This is how time unties to loop through itself, and this is what poems can do.

Away from Tokyo's compression, up in the mountains, we visited Hirashimizu to see its distinctive pottery. Bits of iron in the clay bloom when fired, resulting in characteristic speckles.

We met a potter constructing his own wood-fired kiln even though his workshop already has two enormous gas kilns. It was his day off but there he was, working alone, laying brick and checking levels of level. Asked when he thought it would be finished, the potter only wavered his head and smiled.

> The shrine's cedar trees
> run alongside the kiln site
> making it sacred.
> The process of building
> is the process of being.

꙳

Yamadera, the common name for the complex of temples called Risshaku-ji, was originally built in 860 amid cedar trees and rough stone outcrops. It was here that Basho wrote a famous haiku about the sound of cicadas penetrating the rock in his travel diary *Narrow Road to the Interior.*

trying to calm down
following Basho's footsteps,
I count syllables

✧

a dragonfly lands
on blue hydrangeas
—I'm glad I'm with you

✧

sit and rest with me
in Yamadera's deep shade
Basho and Sora

🙿

We walked through the small town of Yamadera, bought *sembei* (rice crackers) for the train ride, then crossed the bridge with vermillion railings before hoofing it up the far hillside. There, the Yamadera Basho Memorial Museum was built to commemorate the 300th anniversary of Basho's visit to the temple region. A museum, for a poet! I heard that one movie shown there tries to convey the feeling of his trip on foot through this region while another film parallels Basho's wanderings with Saigyo's (1118–1190). I wanted to stand right beside paper the poet had brushed his words on and gaze at his ink-tendrils, but there was no English translation in the museum, so I knew my frustration would be greater to be that close and not comprehend.

Basho Museum—
cicadas in cherry trees
are hurting my ears

Kamakura

After the vast stillnesses of the Japan's north country, we traveled back through Tokyo and Yokohama to spend the day in Kamakura. The stations were crowded; I felt like a rock in a powerful stream. I did catch wonderfully enigmatic English, like the woman's T-shirt that read, "Juicy Culture" or the young man's encouraging us to "Locate Blissful Graph." Freshness Burger was just up the street from Pub Twinkle. The sporting-goods store Golf Paradise had the slogan "meet together and enjoy our golf-style."

On trains, it's easy to see that Japan is mostly mountains. Most people live around river deltas or where the elevation levels off. Just a little way out of any major city, though, are farms and villages.

> black plastic trash bags
> might frighten the crows away—
> not my hungry eyes

ॐ

As in daily life, we must decide what to give ourselves to. We can't avoid picking and choosing. When traveling, we sort options and decide on a plan to avoid aimlessness; on the other hand, wandering enables unanticipated discoveries. Either way, how can I learn to delight in the experience at hand and so drink the antidote to a life of regret?

In Kamakura, we decided to focus on a single Zen temple then walk the Daibutsu Hiking Course through the hills to the Great Buddha before visiting Hasedera with its 30 foot statue of Kannon, the Bodhisattva of Mercy. The slower pace and more solitary approach suit us; taking in too much without time for reflection wears me down and blurs impressions, like running a hand over freshly inked words.

> her finger outstretched
> points out a butterfly—
> one more lands on it

> ✧

> under straw sandals
> larger than any I've seen
> —a green grasshopper

❧

Engaku-ji, the Zen temple, was impressive, not because of its massive two-story San-mon, or main gate (though we did snap pictures of it), and not because of its enormous bell forged in 1301 (though we did climb the 133 steps just to see it), and not because its Buddha relic shrine is a National Treasure, but for the reverence of the place.

The signs that read "Private" or "Keep Out" barring us from buildings or whole areas indicated that this was a place where Buddhism was being practiced. The grounds' reverence seemed a presence in and of itself.

> quiet teaching hall—
> as I step toward the Buddha
> his eyes search me out

❧

Instead of the shrine dedicated to Hachiman, the God of War whose summer grasses grow thick, we found our way through woods on the Hiking Course where our only companions were birds and cicadas. We got turned about and ended up standing gratefully in front of two vending machines, selling cold drinks. A stranger set us straight, down the road, to a tangle of wooden *torii* gates. The shrine to Benten, the Goddess of Peace and Prosperity, was a natural bowl in the hills. Small shrines, complete with bridges short enough to stride across in four steps, were pressed against high walls. A narrow waterfall, no thicker than my arm, made a cooling music.

What draws nearly a million visitors a year is the central cave, the Money-Washing Shrine, where coins are rinsed in the presence of Benten to bring her blessing. I ran water over five-yen coins to give to friends back home.

> the Goddess' cave—
> dripping from the stone ceiling
> strings of folded cranes

࿇

What is it about foxes that awakens the human imagination? Aesop made his fox leap at grapes dangling just out of reach, while in Japan the fox is the messenger of the God of the Harvest, Inari. Since a good rice crop ensures the health of the nation, this communication is important enough to raise shrines all over the country. I always wanted to see one of these *Inari Jinja* (Fox Shrine), to make myself available to such fundamental forces, but like foxes themselves, the experience eluded me all the years I lived in Hiroshima.

I was thrilled, then, to see the stack of vermilion *torii* gates, to climb the stairs from one animal statue to the next, and to stand before the 800-year-old Fox Shrine, Sasuke Inari, in the calm shade of Kamakura. There were hundreds of white porcelain figures, offerings left by pilgrims and others, symbols of human longing deeper than words.

> the shrine's caretaker
> with squirrel photos behind him
> sells me fox figures

✧

> in the forest shade
> we pause to feel the quiet
> —slapping mosquitoes

✧

> beyond the foxes
> the trail drove up, up, uphill
> —sweat drips down my back

❧

The Daibutsu Hiking Course dumped us beside a highway humming with diesel trucks and countless cars. We followed signs to the Great Buddha, cast in bronze in 1252. Even in seated meditation pose, the statue is about fifty feet tall and ninety-seven feet around at the base. Shortly after being finished, rumors of its daunting size reached a whale, who became jealous and demanded to see for himself. The whale donned magic boots and walked ashore, but it could not squeeze itself into the building the statue was then housed in. A priest came out and—with surprising aplomb—asked the whale its business. "I want to know the Daibutsu's height and girth." With that, the statue rose from its meditation, stepped off its pedestal, stood before the whale, and consented to be measured. The priest, using his Buddhist prayer beads, measured both and found the great sea creature was two inches taller and wider. Also, the whale found more respect and humility welling up within him for the great Buddha. I never saw the Daibutsu as much as flinch even with all the photo flashes and people paying ¥20 to climb around inside it.

> we watch each other:
> cameras to our faces
> backs to the Buddha

ଈ

Our day began to feel like more like a pilgrimage, a sacred but austere journey, one that added fasting to the walk from temple to temple; we hadn't had a meal but still had further to go on the Walking Course. After trying to find within me the stillness and concentration I witnessed at the Great Buddha, we strolled to Hasedera to see its Kannon statue, which was carved in 721 and is as tall as five people standing foot to shoulder.

Kannon, the Buddhist figure of compassion, is sometimes depicted with many arms, each ready to save. Sometimes she simply holds a lotus flower to say that beauty and purity are possible even rising from the swamp of one's life and within this world's muck. The Hasedera Kannon is shown with smaller heads emerging from the top of hers, each one inclined to people's cries. In her right hand is a walking staff, as if she's ready to set off at any moment to be of assistance.

As I stepped toward the altar, bit by bit, Kannon was revealed; the ceiling seemed to rise, bringing forth Kannon's neck and mouth, her ears, then her entire head—the figure seemed to go on beyond the room's capacity. When the full statute was before me, and I before it, I was stunned, breathless, and could only pray.

❧

Grace and discipline. Compassion and wisdom. The two feet of spiritual pilgrimage, stepping through the self and through life.

In Kamakura, I stood before the manifestations of these principles. There's a saying that "when Kannon arises in your mind, you are one with Kannon." I hope to engage in the first task of compassion-work: learning through disciplined practice to call it to mind so that it arises naturally and spontaneously.

> boy riding a bike
> covers his face with his hand—
> the sun gets him too

> ✧

> at the hot bus stop
> a stranger gives me iced tea
> —I drink the whole glass

❧

Lost in Gardens

From Kamakura, we seemed to travel back in time when we headed to Kyoto, the ancient capital. However, its train station complex is a futuristic atrium of glass and steel that faces the Kyoto Tower, a needle in the sky. We only had a single day, so all we wanted to do was have another pottery moment, visit Kiyomizudera (one of the most famous temples overlooking the city), and then stand beside or even within a Zen garden.

It was Saturday. Though it's an UNESCO site of world importance, Kiyomizudera had little English for us, and the throngs of visitors seemed especially busy. A woman on her knees praying before the Buddha must have had to concentrate hard amid the chatter, giggles, and photos.

The dry stone garden at Nanzen-ji was an oasis. Grooved lines in white gravel led inward to the heart which can also become grooved with attention and beauty. We sat a long while without words.

> glad for Nanzen-ji
> after all the photo-phones
> at Kiyomizudera

✧

> Tiger? What Tiger?
> Rocks are still rocks. Something
> something moves there.

Maybe it was the heat. Sun relentless on the side of my head, like a hot metal plate. Maybe it was days of profound openness, each new place revealing itself to us. Maybe it was our traveling pace—wake in new room (often before the alarm), check out, haul bags to the train station to stow them in a locker, manage whatever transportation's necessary to view some amazing thing or other, negotiate meals, rush back to the station to catch the incredibly precise bullet train to the next city where we'd stumble into a new room and begin again.

Where is the division between habit that deepens awareness and routine that dulls it? Where's the line between remarkable freshness that delights and numbing innovation?

Somewhere, we'd crossed it.

We were in Takamatsu to stroll Ritsurin, reported to be one of the most beautiful gardens in Japan, but we were numb and dull, cranky and tired.

> Takamatsuya-
> maderamentality—
> lost in translation
>
> ✧
>
> cicadas cry—
> behind the run-down hotel
> there must be some trees
>
> ✧
>
> up at 5:30
> still sleepy but on the train—
> farmers in their fields

🙠

Matsuyama

Our sour mood in Takamastu mixed with pouring rain, so we were glad to board the train for Mastuyama. I wanted to see the childhood home of Masaoka Shiki, the poet who transplanted haiku into the twentieth century so it could flower again. Though he died coughing blood in his thirties, Shiki brought freedom to haiku, and Japanese culture honors him for it. In a room at the top floor of Dogo Hot Spring, a painting shows the novelist Natsume Soseki in a dapper western suit talking with Shiki in Japanese dress—two writers, still friends, in the green fields of the Everlasting. Matsuyama's the only place I know of with a Haiku Post where anyone can submit their poems; good ones are rewarded with some souvenir. I was eager to join the conversation.

> from Yamadera
> to Matsuyama Station—
> the way of haiku

✧

> running for a tram
> I think of Shiki's pained breath—
> lungs like red flowers

☙

Shiki's home, now a museum, was so small. I could feel the seed-like concentration of attentiveness, the sharpness of focus—one persimmon, a cluster of grapes, seventeen syllables. His writing desk sat in front of the *tokonoma,* a small alcove for displaying a hanging scroll and maybe some flowers. Shiki would kneel before it, take up his brush, dip it into black calligraphy ink, and see if details could reach beyond themselves. In front of the house a statue shows him kneeling to tie his shoes, a traveling bundle beside him, ready to set off from his home.

    who will take notice
    a foreign man counting
    beside Shiki's house?

    ✧

    Shiki's childhood home
    makes me think of the man
    —lonely desk and brush

    ✧

    at Dogo Onsen
    I never saw trumpet vines
    just a scrawny cat

☙

We didn't bother with Matsuyama Castle because of the heat. Under the full weight of the sun, who wants to climb an exposed hill to get views obscured by summer's haze? Instead, we hopped a bus for Tobe, the pottery town outside the city. Let off on the side of a road with no sign indicating shops or studios or even clay, we wandered across a river then up the main road determined to ask at the first main building we came to. It turned out to be a family's shop.

A lively old man stepped right up to us and started up, in Japanese. Our stares must have indicated we followed none of it. He asked, still in his language "Do you understand?" We answered with one of the few Japanese phrases we knew, "Sukoshi," meaning "A little." It turned out to be enough for him because he launched into what seemed like his usual sales pitch, at one point placing two handleless cups on the top of the glass display case and rammed one against the other. *Get it? It's strong!*

After we made our purchases, his daughter who did speak some English stepped outside to show us a studio where we could make our own Tobe-yaki, then pointed out where we'd catch our bus back. We didn't try our hand at the wheel, but walked around town a bit. Once ready to return, we got confused and watched as bus after bus pass us, each labeled for destinations we could not read. We waited between the river and the road, the metal guardrail at our calves. All the while the mid-day heat grew; in our bags were empty cups.

>   I've grown so thirsty
>   walking black and white sidewalks
>   —the river's gravel

>   having missed our bus
>   we stand beside the blacktop
>   —the sound of water

a flock of schoolkids
zooms by on their bicycles
—they fly in summer

she stands with a hose
as if she could break the heat
watering her walk

The Heights of Ishizuchi

We rode the earliest train for an hour then a bus that zig-zagged up a river valley. The steep walls rose out of the Omogo-kei gorge then layered back out of sight as if we were being driven through a *sumi-e* painting. Each moment in transit shrank us. Eventually, we were left off in a town which was just an alley of closed shops. The gateway to Ishizuchi, the mountain of accomplishment, as the pamphlet told us, once climbed by Kobo Daishi in 797. He founded the Shingon school of Buddhism in Japan, developed the Japanese alphabet, and wandered the country so far and wide that he is like the pine trees.

From the small town, we caught the gondola up to the first stage of our hike. Through the back windows of the gondola, the loops of wires and huge pylons seemed to march down an increasingly steep slope. We gazed until the drop-off got so intense our stomachs lurched and we had to turn away. The only other passenger was a postman who, upon arrival, promptly strapped his load on and set off. We didn't see any houses all day. We wandered away from the terminal and examined the map with no English, resolved to just keep going uphill.

The highest mountain on the island of Shikoku, Ishizuchi was reserved for pilgrims until relatively recently. And for "pilgrims" read "males only." The trail began with steep switchbacks, then it became stairs or washboards that were like leaning ladders. Ahead, we knew, we faced chains to help haul ourselves up the sharpest inclines. When we read that there were chains, we pictured a kind of pullrope, only sturdier. Maybe loops of cable strung between fence posts, a smaller version of the pylons and gondola wires.

No. These chains laid flat on the rock face, which was steep enough to nearly be a wall. Rings linked together, thick as ladder rungs. How do we make use of these things? Should we climb them by trying to fit our toes in the loops? As we stood, puzzled, a group of pilgrims came huffing up from below. They were keeping quite a pace, and one larger fellow was sweating and red-faced from the effort in unremitting heat. The nimblest took to the chain, straddled it and hunched over, then nearly on all fours, she pulled with her hands and pushed with her toes. Zip, zip, zip—and she was out of sight above us! The others followed more deliberately but were likewise quickly gone. We took our time, afraid our feet would slide out, flattening us against the rock, dangling from our hand grips. But we made it.

At our lunch spot at the top of yet another flight of steep steps, we watched mist move like water, flowing through valleys and surging up toward us like a silent tide pouring in. It turned peaks into islands in a churning white-grey sea. Now I know why people believe the gods took up residence in the mountains. Saigyo wrote nearly a thousand years ago that he followed "the paths the gods passed over" and that he sought "their innermost place." Though a millennia separate us, we are companions on this journey.

Those clouds brought rain, water streaming from the brims of our hats. We had no umbrellas or other gear for such a storm. And then we heard thunder.

> in remote mountains
> mist-spirits through the pine forest—
> the gods' flowing robes

꙳

When I Say 'Hiroshima'

If the first part of our travels were as pilgrims moving from place to place, the second part was a journey of the heart. We'd remain in one place, and travel deeply.

We were going to Hiroshima, to commemorate events of the past and renew friendships after ten years. To get there from Matsuyama, Beth and I spent a few delightful hours on the ferry across the Seto Inland Sea. We could have splurged on a faster ship, but we appreciated the pace of the commuter ferry. On the slower boat, time felt like a luxury compared to the speed and efficiency of the bullet trains.

Though the day was humid and hot, the vessel parted the sea air. Islands like blue mountains floated in the haze. We caught up on our journals, ate lunch, and rested. Drawing close to Ujina, Hiroshima's port, we recognized the Prince Hotel—in our final week in Hiroshima, our friend Taeko gifted us with one extravagant night. We both teared up at the memory.

> in the engine's noise
> and the sway of the ferry
> a calm solitude

✧

> Seto Sea's islands—
> towns on the coast like gravel
> washed down from mountains

✧

> the ferry boat docks,
> engines rumbling, water white—
> brooms sway on hooks

❦

The World Friendship Center, the peace organization we volunteered for, hosted us all week to mark the 60th year since the atomic bomb leveled Hiroshima. Having lived inside that story for two and a half years, I didn't expect to be moved. The official ceremony on August 6 was the usual parade of politicians mouthing predictable things. None of the survivors we knew ever attend.

But on the morning of the fourth, we attended a ceremony at the Memorial of the A-bombed Teachers and Students of National Elementary Schools. The trees were already loud with cicadas at 8 a.m. The screws of heat had already begun to turn and press down. Camera crews crouched to get the right angle of the mayor and various education officials who spoke, but the heart of the ceremony was the line of children who came forward when their school was called to make offerings at the foot of the statue: a dramatic figure of a woman—a teacher—trying to carry a child in her arms but her fatigue is great and the small body's weight is too much. The child is slipping . . .

> tolling the school names
> they offer flowers and cranes
> —they were just children

❦

Seeing our friends again showed us how bonds that deep don't wear away. It is a chain under the ground of our lives, securing each of us to the earth.

Yoko met us at the port then said abruptly, "I need to talk with you . . . Shall we get some coffee?" The dread that arises when those words are spoken gave way to happiness as I realized that she was merely saying that she needed to talk to us—it had been years! And so, we spent hours in the overly air-conditioned bakery laughing over our many joys working together.

Itsue rode her bike to our hotel at 10 p.m. because she couldn't wait until the next day to see us. She gave me a book of the Heart Sutra, which she chants each day, because "form is emptiness, emptiness is form." She knows that what is not here is never gone.

Before we knew Okoshi-san's name, we called the noodle shop owner "The Geta Man" because he wore traditional Japanese wooden clogs. It was his idea to go on a dinner cruise in the Seto Sea, an extravagance he arranged and one we never experienced when we lived a few blocks from it. A few days later, after closing his shop he treated us to lunch of his noodles; he even offered to give me the very bowl I was eating out of because it was made in Tobe.

Taeko welcomed us into her house, saying, "It's very *HOT*" because her house was not air-conditioned. "But if you know that, it's not as hot," she noted, sagely. We drank cool *mugicha,* roasted barley tea, and talked as if we would walk home and see her again the next day. Just as we would a decade before.

>after all these years
>when I say Hiroshima
>it means "home"

❧

Shu's muscular body seemed small behind Machiko's wheelchair, especially when he leaned it back, back, far back until the front wheels caught the edge of the stage. Rin was wearing a metal necklace that chimed when she bent to speak to Machiko. Shu and Rin and Machiko were to give us a prayer song at the World Friendship Center's Welcome Party, but first Shu held up a square box—the thumb harp! I recognized it immediately. He told the audience how Beth and I had presented that very instrument to him ten years ago and in the meantime, music had taken his life in new directions. Music even carried the three of them to Africa! They started a rhythmic melody on thumb harps then let their voices lead them, lead us all through a passage we could only find by feel.

We had dinner with the three of them. Sitting by the river where evening's breezes blew cool and steady, we caught up on their journey to Niger and how music lit the way for Shu through the darkness after his cancer-laced difficulties. They played another song that I remembered from rice-harvest parties in Shiraki-cho, ten autumns before. The song smelled of sake and wood smoke.

On the evening of August 6th, with colorful lanterns floating and peace pilgrims gathering, they played again on the banks of the Motoyasu River. Facing the skeletal Atomic Bomb Dome, they started with voices and thumb-harps, while Shu's mouth-harp buzzed out a rhythm. It was the authentic gesture I had been longing for all day. I didn't know I was so hungry for such a moment until the feast of it was offered. Throughout the day, Peace Park seemed more like a festival, but now with the dark gathering around us, the whole memorial space was a sacred circle, the spirits had been invoked and invited to follow the currents home.

> the motion of peace
> drifts over the river
> —just their two voices.

☙

Hiroshima has its own poets. Kurihara Sadako, whom I was fortunate enough to meet once on the street while she, in her eighties, wore a sign protesting nuclear power, wrote "Let us be midwives! / Let us be midwives! / Even if we lay down our lives to do so." Sankichi Toge has a memorial in Peace Park inscribed with his plea to gain our humanity back after targeting whole cities. "Give back my father, give back my mother." His poem never uses words like "A-bomb" or "atomic" or else the US occupation would have censored him. Under the stone, his pen is buried like a seed. Morishita Hiromu wrote a poem asking us to listen to Hiroshima not just with your ears, not just "with your arm or with your head. / With the heart of one who endures despair."

Time is strange. The amount of it only measured two weeks, but its scope and depth and heft of these encounters made it so much more. Like a poem, the richness of experience suspends and expands our lives. In this way, Japan got inside me. We carry the landscape, the trains, and our friends home with us—not just photo albums or images in mind, but part of our blood and breath, mysteriously resident in our heartbeat.

REGROUNDING

*Home is the sum of all
The days that shelter us*

—Kathleen Raine

Grace Street (II)

It started with Gary
Snyder, his mind-
direct road cuts.

        Black locust
so late to leaf
    I thought it damaged.
          Mowing the back yard,
    I stopped for the already-
down branch, took it in, filling vases.
        Evenings,
    sweetness
hung like healing gauze.

In *Back Country,* Snyder starts
in America's Northwest,
sails west to reach Far East
    —like us, like us—
    I recognized
    Mrs. Yamade in his lines
*cuts down the tall spike weeds—
    more in two hours
than I can get done in a day.*

Only now, by the highway
in our Yellow House on Grace Street
summer beginning
its long drone
    do I feel myself returning.

◊   *Beginnings*   ◊

All winter-into-spring, I spent
with Muriel Rukeyser, mother Muriel,
hoping to read my way
into some direction, some means of arrival

where? each question *what should I do?*
is driven by longings for permanence.
As we moved, each box
                —old journals & letters, sheetmusic,
    cassettes, projects-half-done
        or undone, Japanese mementos—
became a dustburst
until everything settled into its place,

devising systems to order them,
system which always break down.
Still, beginnings are essential.

And still, through it all, there was Muriel
saying   *one opens, yes,*
          and one's life keeps opening.

◊   *Tilling*   ◊

Rains came, then wind.
The locust tree, that fountain
of fragrance, let its petals
flurry across the garden.
Grass was a thick mat,
even with two tillings, soil
like lumber. And the rocks!
Bill (trying to shake Wild
from his name) at Tanglewood
said, "they think anything
not shale is soil."
Then in the breeze:
cotton. *Know roots,*
Roethke advises. With soft toes,
I gripped the earth.

◊   *The Bear*   ◊

Like wrestling a bear, wrestling
three your size, three
of your own grizzly selves,
powerful but playful—
won't use claws.
At the crossroads of our return:
job-choices aren't just
questions of a paycheck.
                Take heed . . .
    Promptings of Love and Truth
in your hearts are the leadings of God.

In such a wrangle
we can be *heard* into realizations.
Douglas Steere:
> *To 'listen' another's soul*
> > *into disclosure and discovery*
> *may be the greatest service any*
> > *human being ever performs for another.*

But the she-bear! A part of you
feels torn away. The grief-growl,
paw-swipes at territory borders.
All through these weeks
every other phone call
reviewed the choices. Pros, cons
(On the *other* other hand . . .)
and your mother pressing for answers:
will we visit
and if so
would we want to go white water rafting?

Self-possession's wild work.

The only relief—
digging corn rows, planting sunflowers,
Shasta daisies, and cosmos in the far bed
—work for another season.

Don gave us two Russian tomato plants
he raised from seed.

◊ *Sentencing* ◊

The beans came up   the death verdict
came down   Our best guess   from Rodale's *Controlling*
Pests and Diseases: Cabbage Maggot   So I turn again
to the old physician   To embrace this earth
The only universal is the local   Old Doc Williams says
Is that why the sentence of death   so elated so many
Our homegrown bomber   (his name passes here
with him back to soil) breathed his "Invectus"
into the air of America   and at Agway
when we asked about the beans   we were shown
immediately the insecticide aisle   Problem → solution
If → then   Inevitable.

Why do I write today?

> *The beauty of*
>   *the terrible faces*
>   *of our nonentities*
>   *stirs me to it . . .*

okay   Williams makes me uneasy
with all that talk of young girls   and their thighs
but starlings   chicory and daisies   a severed cod
memory fading in a failing body
that red firetruck   plunging through the dark city
and all those Brueghels   all of it   he received all of it

so openly so freely   *All because the poem*
                           is . . . the secret
                  at the heart of the matter
                     for integrity of understanding
                                to insure
                           persistence,
                                to give the mind its stay.

◊   *Secret Agents*   ◊

"Bacteria are the agents
of the transformation . . ."

   Down to one
   bag of garbage a week;
         even fewer
      if we get
the compost pile steaming.

"Once I began to cooperate with nature,
my soil improved quickly."

◊   *Backyard Wisdom*   ◊

All wisdom is rooted in learning
to call things by the right name.
                    —Confucius

Finally, I'm sorting out
some of the poplars: what Arnie called
Mormon Trees, those "water-sucking,
upright-standing,
no-shade-giving trees"
are Lombardy Poplars, cultivated
in Europe before Handel died in 1759.
Now only males are planted.

Yellow Poplar is a kind of
magnolia, called Tuliptree
because of its upright flowers.
I haven't seen one nearby
but my attention's been on

the Cottonwoods filling
the air with white blessings.
Kunitz says *a poet*
needs to keep his wilderness
alive inside him. Related to Aspen
(but not Birches) Eastern Cottonwoods
can grow thirteen feet the first year.

Don't know why Don calls it Popple
but am glad I painted the deck when I did.

◊ *Bolt* ◊

End
of June. Close up
the house against heat.
Lettuce
about to bolt.

Between Mothers
and Fathers Day,
it sprang up.
So tasty
those leaves.

◊ *A Hard Rain* ◊

Not only boxes but too much
furniture, bookcases, stereo stuff
—then we bought new machines
that seem so essential.
And so, I read Rexroth,

poems as smooth as garden stones.
We've had guests and trips, all taking us
from ourselves. And now
you're starting the BOCES job,
learning its politics

—all before we drive (again)
to Atlanta for July Fourth.

Like sudden thundershowers,
sometimes life pelts down
too fast, too hard to really soak in.
I better turn the compost well.

Rexroth is just a man speaking, but one
who learned an early lesson
and worked it out traveling,
working, writing: *Life*
    must be lived nobly
        and to the utmost;
      each must realize something
    out of his or her existence:
      'a flame,
        a jewel,
            a splendour.'"

WIDE MIGRATIONS

*Every spirit builds itself a house;
and beyond its house a world;
and beyond its world, a heaven.*

—Emerson

False Spring

We walked to the hillcrest
where the solar system
stood a moment underfoot.

Patches of snow and ice
reshaped themselves
into the pond twenty yards
downhill. Sparrows
sprang across the openness
weaving an invisible cloth.

In our coats, the wind
returned to the blue house,
the one with no secrets.

Forsythia

Walking through open rooms
cradling her newborn,
a pang like a staple
went through her then locked.

She gazed into her infant's face
and knew her daughter
was considering the end
of the world. *What kind of mother
am I,* she asked herself,
to think this? She won't
speak of it but knows

one day the girl
will ask the forsythia hedge
"when will the men
and women all die," and it
will answer *I am green now.
That is all I know.*

Strange Visitor

after a painting by Willi Schiener

Playing the waves, a surfer had his board
snapped in half. Four dolphins nosed
the huge sharks away.

>Maybe we should
>be grateful. Blue
>with gratitude. Blue
>as the sea looks
>from space.

On the trip to Mystic Aquarium, the kids
knew: the sea show, though cut short
by dolphin antics, was the day's prize.

>In the depths, yellow
>is hot. Barrels
>painted in code colors
>as if marine animals
>could read:
>*slow death.*

When the dolphins washed up, dead,
on the Jersey shore, people panicked.
The blood line being short between mammals.

>Green-blue sea lit by wide light.
>Grey dolphins hear the thing
>break the surface,
>and swim to meet it.
>They approach
>as if to ask
>*Who are you?*
>The mute barrel sinks.

In the Desert

for Mary Hood

—i—

These ripening summer mornings, the light's
up early, and today Bach's on the rise—
all those intervals and filigrees. A woman
who delighted in counterpoint
left the conservatory for the biology lab
exchanging one pattern-search for another
and ended up studying ants—pheromones
like a fugue. In an ant colony, she said,
no one is in charge.

—ii—

Do travelers in the unknown
see it all as just not-yet-
figured-out? A problem
to solve? Where is the *mysterium*

tremendum that sets us quaking,
trembling like aspen leaves
under the influence of forces
greater than and beyond us?

—iii—

From the deserts of Kazakhstan,
the arid lands of Mongolia
the rain shadow region of the Gobi,

yellow dust plumes to drift
over coastal China, Korea,
the Japan Sea, even the Pacific.

Though inanimate, the earth
is on the move. And now,
though tiny, particles like sherpas

bear microscopic burdens
of cadmium and other metals,
so small, so small, and yet

an officewoman in Kamakura
or a schoolkid in Portland
can breathe them in, and

still traveling, they can pass
right through cellular membranes
into the blue waterways of the blood.

—*iv*—

We are thirsty,
so parched
with knowledge,

so dry with thirst.
And that well
is so salty.

Where is the spring,
the fresh water?
Where is the source

of hope? How can we
trust the future
we are making?

Listen, listen—
the patterns
are not complete.

Mending the Earth

after a photo creation by Robert Parke Harrison

The solitary man
crouches to his task,

his one hand on the crack
that stretches beyond him
and far beyond our sight.

What wound, what scar
is yours to heal?

Could the Earth
be the object
of such affection?

In the bleak of December—
forsythia in freak bloom.

What scars the heart?
The needle's as big
as the man. Like a sigh,

a white cloud
issues from the fissure.

He's stitched only a little.
His thick thread
will run out.

A Poem With No One in It

At the water's edge, the sun
presses its solid weight.
A shadow of small fish

negotiates the current,
turning against it first
then rolling with it

swiftly curling into
and around an eddy
where they gather in a tight knot.

Warm water. Granite
holding the flow, pink,
orange, green with lichen.

Wind down the creekbed
cool, like the long wings
of the heron, opening.

The Search for Avalon

Night air pimples the skin.
Sun bright, but not yet warm.
A flock of sandpipers starts
and moves off together
like a ghost. The spirit
longs for Avalon, a place
some say doesn't even exist,

except in the mind (as the body
houses the heart, Spirit
houses us all). Yet some
will swim the treacherous channel,
battling shifting tides to shipwreck
on its secret, fulfilling shores.

Then at dawn, before most wake,
when sand is cold under bare feet
and wind speaks
with night's heavy accent,
the waves in their constant motion
wash and wash you
in the mercy of the world.

Real Spring

In the yard, tenderness followed
an arc of rain, gone overnight.
Like stalks of fireworks, crocuses,
white and gold, shot out
above the leaf-strewn mat.

Behind the crab-apple, all sticks
and rough bark—the flutter and jabber
of robins. Something gentle
is breaking open,
something wild.

The Circuit

The lilac is still green down
to its twiggy heart. At 3,
we agreed, we'd go visit
the yard. But first:
nose to the grindstone
(that lie that unravels).

Then Dave dropped by.
His floppy eared
Beagle-lab pup
is all sniffer and paws.

Out back, the linden
stands in a grey circle
of its own crispy leaves.

Up through the soil, between
the pine's needles
surges the oceanic and continual.
My breath is tidal.
I float the large current
out over the cemetery,
the dike and river, the highway,
factory, and power station.

The journey, the wide migration
of all living things
is through air and water
through earth and fire
through variations
and the hidden wholeness.

The sporadic flutter
of a chickadee's wings
calls me back
to a familiar half-acre,
home in the grain
of a grassblade.

For the Autumn Equinox

—i—

All that rain.
And darkness. Soon
the golden leaves

of the locust trees
will drift
into the blindness

of snow. All the broadcast talk
of what's not working.
All that anger. *Resentment,*

says Augustine,
*is a metal poker fired
red-hot in the heart.*

*To scorch another
you must first
wound yourself.*

What is it
you need
to begin healing?

—ii—

Beginning this
the 267th day of the year
    as the leaves
yellow and the air sharpens

I release the little kingdoms
of personal striving. Today
    I begin
by watching the dawn.

—*iii*—

Because in her beautiful hands
my love took oranges, sliced them
to reveal their sectioned dawns,
squeezed out their pulpy juice

then made a gift

of far away groves, a distant
warmth, a season long gone,

I drink the memory
of blue sky. These days
when the sky is lead
hammered flat—appearing
        as close overhead
        as on the far side of sight
in the thinning dark,
I drink the sun.

The half-moon orange peels
I cram into the compost heap.

—iv—

Remembering begins delight

Even the bitter rinds
(when offered properly)
nourish beans, tomatoes,

the clinging vine
of squash, and around the edges
to shine
on all that grows

on stalks as firm
as metal poles

sunflowers

—v—

Under a sickle moon, smiling
just bright enough to make out
the lumpy O of its body,

day ripens. Today
light and dark embrace
and are equals.

Spruce Trees in Rain

Today, the dark curtains
of the spruce trees reveal
rain in beaded streaks.
Those beings teach me
the meaning of resilience,
how to stay green, receiving
like communion what light
there is, regardless of season;
to sway in high winds, hanging
loose and limber, bending
as needed to remain upright;
to grow great in unseen regions,
and draw nourishment
in darkness, from darkness;
to shelter the living and the dead;
to live as witness, as sentinel.
Today in rain, the spruce trees
drip from ten thousand needles—
all that motion, all that liquid,
and walking beneath them, I remain
dry, robed in green silence.

Autumn Songs

Startling, the sky's color
burns with insistence, unafraid,
unoccupied by any arguments
or approaching darkness.

Once again, the range of blue
convinces, saying *autumn,* saying
things hold their own ending.

Spruce trees, in their deep green, say
the season bears a redeeming stamp.

A goldfinch—a song, a riddle,
a beautiful slightness
                out of the eastern sky—sings
            you are soft clay
                ready for the fire.

Listening to Snow

—i—

Not a tight-tethered
              kite, but floating.
           Like leaves
crackling dry to any wind. There it goes,
slipping like a stream of egg-white
into boiling water, a part of me
through a soul-seam.
I want to lean like a stone wall,
weathered.
            No words. No gestures.
Ice closing its gates in shaded shelves.
Against such cold, I hunch against the world.
Early and long
            the dark comes on.
Along the frozen creek, along its rocky bank,
leaves scuttle in a terrible emptiness.

—ii—

Work bends me to face
tabletops and pools
of paper

a journey into others' lives

Leaves plume as if out of the ground
and when I look
the engine starts

the whole building slides forward

A passenger now
I gaze at stationary clouds
the motion fierce within me

—iii—

Night's lengthening becomes
                              a weariness,
slowness
       of soul; it makes
bearing one more phrase
                     too much. Too many
faces in a fog-shut day.
                    Doors slam,
their metal voices reproaching.

—iv—

> *waiting for dandelions to break into song*
>   —John Bradley

Atop the dark load
in its basket, a cardboard box
holds seeds in white envelopes.
Peppers, green beans, eggplants.

Already in the house,
tiny lavender flowers.
Snow keeps falling:
fragments of a spotlight.
The air is tangled
with birdsong.
The snow whispers
*I'm swelling
the Chesapeake.*

—v—

Mostly, I stay:

a sign, a spindle of shale,
a roadside teasel
snowcapped.

Sometimes I push
the earth, but night passes
in mercy, with mercy

stars fall, white blurs
streaking past me,
through me.

Snowfields

—i—

Behind the leafless
wayfinding of the bushes,

morning light's
an effortless presence,

best received.
Snow on spruce

and cedar branches—
light-flecks

rising to snow-clouds,
a vague limit, a seal
on the horizon.

—ii—

In the season of darkness,
mornings lift, snowlight rises
all around at once—
white clapboard,
white deck rail
fading into fields of white
on ground, on pool cover, and up
up on furred linden branches.

—iii—

All emerges from within:
this soft white field,
this effortless presence,

this hospitality,
this expansive
identity—

the movement, where
being and becoming
never end.

For the Winter Solstice

I bathe myself in winter's
brief light the color
of dusted snow.
In the pool of warmth
around your body,
I sleep. Passion
true enough
to cleanse. My love,

I remember the yellow blessing
of candle light
on your sleeping face.

When morning comes,
it will be time
to rise, now rested, and
enter winter again. Time
to give light.

About the Author

Edward A. Dougherty graduated from Penn State with a BA in English and worked for a few years before moving to Bowling Green, Ohio, to pursue an MFA. He and the love of his life devoted two and a half years to volunteering for peace as the directors of the World Friendship Center in Hiroshima, Japan. To reacclimate to US culture and to discern their next steps, they spent nearly a year at Pendle Hill, the Quaker Center for Contemplation and Study outside of Philadelphia. They now live in the southern Finger Lakes region of upstate New York.

Dougherty is the author of a collection of essays called *Journey Work: Crafting a Life of Poetry and Spirit* (Loyola College/Apprentice House, 2021) and the co-author of *Double Bloom: Exercises for Poets* (Pearson, 2006) with Scott Minar. He has published many collections of poetry, including *Grace Street* (Cayuga Lake Books, 2016) and *10048* (Finishing Line Press, 2019). This book appears the same year as his *Selected Poems* from FutureCycle Press. Dougherty was granted the SUNY Chancellor's Award for Scholarship and Creative Activities.

www.ingramcontent.com/pod-product-compliance
Lightning Source LLC
Chambersburg PA
CBHW022145160426
43197CB00009B/1434